I'M A Python PROGRAMMER

{ BUILD 11 PROGRAMS }

Max Wainewright

Crabtree Publishing Company

www.crabtreebooks.com

Crabtree Publishing Company
www.crabtreebooks.com
1-800-387-7650

Published in Canada
Crabtree Publishing
616 Welland Avenue
St. Catharines, ON
L2M 5V6

Published in the United States
Crabtree Publishing
PMB 59051
350 Fifth Ave, 59th Floor
New York, NY 10118

Published in 2018 by CRABTREE PUBLISHING COMPANY.

First published in 2017 by Wayland
Text copyright © ICT Apps Ltd, 2017
Art and design copyright © Hodder and Stoughton Limited, 2017

Author: Max Wainewright
Editorial director: Kathy Middleton
Editors: Liza Miller, Janine Deschenes
Freelance editor: Hayley Fairhead
Designer: Peter Clayman
Illustrator: Ladiebirdy
Proofreader: Wendy Scavuzzo
Prepress technician: Tammy McGarr
Print and production coordinator: Margaret Amy Salter

Consultant: Lee Martin, B. Ed, E-Learning Specialist

The website addresses (URLs) included in this book were valid at the time of going to press. However, it is possible that contents or addresses may have changed since the publication of this book. No responsibility for any such changes can be accepted by either the author or the Publisher.

E-safety
Children will need access to the Internet for most of the activities in this book. Parents or teachers should supervise this and discuss staying safe online with children.

Printed in the USA/072017/CG20170524

Library and Archives Canada Cataloguing in Publication

Wainewright, Max, author
     I'm a Python programmer / Max Wainewright.

(Generation code)
Includes index.
Issued in print and electronic formats.
ISBN 978-0-7787-3519-9 (hardcover).--ISBN 978-0-7787-3533-5 (softcover).--
ISBN 978-1-4271-1939-1 (HTML)

     1. Python (Computer program language)--Juvenile literature.
2. Computer programming--Juvenile literature. I. Title. II. Title: I am a Python programmer.

QA76.73.P98W36 2017   j005.13'3   C2017-902537-6
                                                C2017-902538-4

Library of Congress Cataloging-in-Publication Data

CIP available at the Library of Congress

CONTENTS

INTRODUCTION

Python is a language that is used by professional programmers. Different programming languages are good at doing different things. Python can create 3-D graphics for special effects in movies, and is often used on web servers to handle searching.

This book contains all the techniques and ideas you need to know to become a Python programming genius! Learn the basics and how to use *loops* and *variables* in Python. Discover how to create graphics, use *random numbers*, and build games, simulations, and other programs.

www.python.org

⠿ python

clock.py

```
def makeFace():
    b=turtle.Turtle()
    b.speed(0)
    b.hide turtle()
    b.penup

    b.dot(350)
    b.pencolor('white')
    b.dot(340)
```

```
>>>
== RESTART: hello.py ===
hello
hello
hello
>>>
```

Before you get started on your programs, you'll need to download and install Python on your computer. Find out how on page 4.

The **IDLE Editor** is where you will be typing your code.

The **Console** is where you will see any text your program outputs—as well as information about any bugs!

The *Turtle* **Graphics** window is where any graphics your program draws will be displayed.

CODE CAREFULLY AND AVOID THE BUGS!

Bugs are errors or mistakes in your code that stop your program from working properly. Looking for these errors is called *debugging*. Make sure you enter your code very carefully. If things aren't working properly, see the tips on page 3l to help you.

Note: Words in *italics* appear in the glossary on page 30.

‹3›

❯ GETTING STARTED

INSTALLING PYTHON

First, you need to make sure that your computer has the software you need to be able to code with Python. Download the newest free version from the Python website. There are some apps for tablets that run Python, but you will need to use a Mac or PC to do most of these activities. (Ask permission from the person who owns your computer before you download the software.)

STEP 1 – FIND THE PYTHON WEBSITE ❯

⇨ Open your web browser and visit **www.python.org**

STEP 2 – START DOWNLOADING ❯

⇨ Click the **Downloads** button near the top of the web page.

⇨ Select a version from the list at the bottom of the page. Different versions of Python may be available for your computer. This book uses Python 3.5. Make sure you choose a version starting with Python 3, not Python 2. For Windows XP or older versions, download Python 3.4.

⇨ Wait for the download to complete.

STEP 3 – INSTALL THE SOFTWARE ❯

⇨ Some browsers will then ask you to run the installation program. Choose **Run**.

⇨ If this doesn't happen, don't panic. The installer file should have been downloaded to your computer. Look in your **Downloads** folder for it. Double-click it to start installing Python. You should get a box giving you instructions on what to do next. Follow them to complete the installation.

STEP 4 – RUN PYTHON ❯

On a PC:
⇨ Click **Start** > **Programs** > **Python** > **IDLE**.
Or just click **IDLE(Python)** if it appears in the "recently added" section.

On a Mac:
⇨ Click **Finder**.
⇨ Click **Applications**.
⇨ Double-click **Python 3**.
⇨ Click the **IDLE** icon.
⇨ Make a shortcut by dragging the **IDLE** file onto your dock at the bottom of the desktop.
⇨ Click the **IDLE** icon.

SAYING HI!

When computer programmers start learning a new language, the first thing they usually do is learn to make a program that displays a message, such as "Hello world". Let's look at how to do that in Python.

HELLO WORLD!

STEP 1 – RUN IDLE

IDLE stands for Integrated Development and Learning Environment. This is the program you will use to create your code. Click the shortcut to **IDLE** on your computer. (See step 4 from page 4.)

STEP 2 – START A NEW FILE

⇨ Click the **File** menu, then choose **New File**.

IDLE **File** Edit

    New File

    Open...

STEP 3 – GET CODING!

⇨ Carefully type in the code shown below:

The brackets tell Python where the item to display starts and ends.

Untitled

```
print('Hello world')
```

The **print** *command* tells Python to display something.

The quotation marks tell Python that the item to display is a **text** *string* (some letters).

You must type your code in exactly! If you leave out a quotation mark or bracket, it will not work. **IDLE** will make parts of your code change color to let you know you have added brackets and quotation marks correctly. Python is **case-sensitive**, which means you need to use lowercase letters for your commands.

STEP 4 – SAVE YOUR CODE

⇨ Click the **File** menu, then choose **Save**.

IDLE **File** Edit

    Open...

    Save...

⇨ Type **hello** as the filename.

⇨ Click **Save**.

STEP 5 – RUN YOUR CODE

⇨ Click the **Run** menu, then choose **Run Module**.

mat **Run** Optio

    Python...

    Run Module

```
>>>
== RESTART: hello.py ===
Hello world
>>>
```

CUSTOMIZE

• Add more lines to your program.

• Can you make it tell a simple story?

• You'll need to save and run your program (steps 4 and 5) each time you add new code.

> LOOPS AND VARIABLES

If you've done some coding before, you will know that one of the most important programming concepts is the loop. If you want your code to do something over and over again, it's much quicker to use a loop instead of copying out the code several times. Let's look at how this works in Python.

STEP 1 – START A NEW FILE

⇨ Run **IDLE**. See step 4 from page 4 if you need help.

⇨ Click the **File** menu, then choose **New File**.

> IDLE **File** Edit
> **New File**
> Open...

STEP 2 – GET CODING!

⇨ Carefully type in this code. Press enter after each line.

> Untitled
> ```
> print('hello')
> print('hello')
> print('hello')
> ```

STEP 3 – SAVE YOUR CODE

⇨ Click **File** > **Save**.

⇨ Type **loops** as the filename.

⇨ Click **Save**.

> IDLE **File** Edit
> Open ..
> Save ..

STEP 4 – RUN YOUR CODE

⇨ Click the **Run** menu, then choose **Run Module**.

> mat **Run** Optio
> Python ..
> **Run Module**

> Python 3.5 Shell
> ```
> >>>
> == RESTART: loops.py ===
> hello
> hello
> hello
> >>>
> ```

STEP 5 – USE A LOOP

Steps 1 to 4 are a simple way to make our program say **hello** three times. But what if you wanted to make it say **hello** ten or a hundred times? There is a quicker way.

⇨ Delete your code and change it to the code shown to the right:

⇨ Check your code carefully for mistakes. **Save** and **Run** your code. What happens?

The **for** command starts the loop.

The commands you want to repeat must be indented. Python should automatically indent lines for you. If it doesn't, just use the space bar or the tab key to indent the code exactly as shown.

a is a variable (see page 7).

The number of times to repeat the loop.

> loops.py
> ```
> for a in range(10):
>     print('hello')
> ```

A colon must be at the end of the line.

Variables are special parts of a program that store data or information.

Variables are different from ordinary numbers because they can be changed as a program runs.

Variables have a name that is used to point to a part of the computer's memory. A value is then stored in that part of the memory.

STEP 6 – KEEPING COUNT

A variable is used in Python to count how many times a **loop** has been repeated. In our program, the variable is called **a**, but it can be given any letter or word as a name. By printing that variable, we can change our program to make it count from 0 to 4.

⇨ Delete and change your code so it says:

loops.py
```
for a in range(5):
    print(a)
```

Look at how the print command has been written. If there were quotation marks around the letter **a**, Python would think it was a text string and would print the letter **a** ten times. But because there are no quotation marks, Python knows **a** is a variable.

Python 3.5 Shell
```
>>>
0
1
2
3
4
>>>
```

⇨ **Save** and **Run** your code to see what happens.

STEP 7 – COUNTING BACKWARD

⇨ Delete and change your code again and insert the extra numbers shown inside the brackets below.

1 3 9 7 2
6 8 5 10 4

The number to start at.

Stop repeating when this number is reached.

Change the number by this amount each time.

loops.py
```
for a in range(10,0,-1):
    print(a)
```

Save and **Run** your code.

CUSTOMIZE
- Try to make your program count down from 100 all the way to 0.
- Pick a times table, such as the five times table. Adapt your code so it counts from 5, 10, 15, 20... up to 60.

KEY CONCEPTS

LOOPS
When we want to repeat some code, we use a loop.

VARIABLES
When we want a number to store a value that will change, we use a variable. In our loop, **a** is a variable.

> TURTLE GRAPHICS

So far, everything we have produced from our code has been text. In this activity, we will look at how we can produce art, or graphics, in Python. To do this, we need to "borrow" a set of commands called the turtle graphics *library*.

STEP 1 – START A NEW FILE ▶

⇨ Run **IDLE**.

⇨ Click the **File** menu, then choose **New File**.

IDLE	**File**	Edit
	New File	
	Open...	

STEP 2 – GET CODING! ▶

⇨ Carefully type in this code:

```
Untitled
import turtle
turtle.fd(100)
```

The command **import turtle** tells Python to borrow the turtle graphics *library* for our program.

turtle.fd(100) means move the turtle forward 100 *steps* in the current direction.

STEP 3 – SAVE YOUR CODE ▶

⇨ Click **File** > **Save**.

IDLE	**File**	Edit
	Open ..	
	Save ..	

⇨ Type **shapes** as the filename.

⇨ Click **Save**.

Make sure you use the name **shapes**. Never give one of your files the name **turtle** or it will confuse Python and stop it from working.

STEP 4 – RUN YOUR CODE ▶

⇨ Click the **Run** menu, then choose **Run Module**.

mat	**Run**	Optio
	Python ..	
	Run Module	

Instead of the normal window, you should see a simple graphics window.

The Python turtle will draw an arrow 100 steps long on the graphics window.

STEP 5 – MORE COMMANDS ▶

⇨ Add more commands to your program.

```
shapes.py
import turtle
turtle.fd(100)
turtle.rt(90)
turtle.fd(100)
```

Python must tell the turtle to change direction before moving forward again. To do this, we use the command **turtle.rt(90)** to turn the turtle 90 *degrees* to the right.

⇨ **Save** and **Run** your code to test out your new commands.

STEP 6 – ALL SQUARE ▶

⇨ Add more commands to draw a square.

```
shapes.py
import turtle
turtle.fd(100)
turtle.rt(90)
turtle.fd(100)
turtle.rt(90)
turtle.fd(100)
turtle.rt(90)
turtle.fd(100)
```

⇨ **Save** and **Run** your code. You should have drawn a complete square!

CUSTOMIZE
- Try to make your square bigger.
- Which numbers need to change, and which need to stay the same?
- Experiment with **turtle.lt(90)**. What does it do?

STEP 7 – CHANGE COLOR ▶

⇨ Delete your existing code and change it to the following:

```
shapes.py
import turtle
turtle.color('red')
turtle.fd(50)
turtle.color('blue')
turtle.fd(50)
```

 ⇨ **Save** and **Run** your code. What does your arrow look like now?

KEY CONCEPT ◀

TURTLE GRAPHICS LIBRARY

The turtle graphics library is a set of commands used to move an object around the screen. As the object moves, it draws lines and patterns.

STEP 8 – TRY TO DRAW ▶

⇨ Make your own shapes and patterns.

⇨ Can you draw your initials, or even your whole name?

> PROGRAMMING POLYGONS

In the previous activity, we started to use turtle graphics to draw things. It is often easier to draw shapes by using loops (see page 6). This is because we can write the code to draw one side of the shape, then repeat that code to draw the other sides.

STEP 1 – CODE A SQUARE ▷

⇨ Run **IDLE** and start a new file.

⇨ Type in this code:

> Indent these two lines so Python knows which lines to repeat.

> Move the turtle forward 100 steps.

⇨ Type **polygons** as the filename.

Prepare the graphics library.

```
Untitled
import turtle
for s in range(4):
    turtle.lt(90)
    turtle.fd(100)
```

Start a loop that repeats four times. (Don't forget the colon!)

Turn the turtle left a quarter turn.

STEP 2 – RUN YOUR CODE ▷

⇨ Click the **Run** menu, then choose **Run Module.**

mat **Run** Optio

Python ..

Run Module

STEP 3 – MAKE AN OCTAGON ▷

⇨ Modify your code so it repeats the loop eight times and turns 45 degrees.

```
polygons.py
import turtle
for s in range(8):
    turtle.lt(45)
    turtle.fd(100)
```

⇨ **Save** and **Run** your code. You've drawn an octagon!

CUSTOMIZE

• Modify your code again to make other polygons. You will need to think about how many times the **for** loop needs to run and the angle it needs to turn:

• A square has 4 sides, so the loop runs 4 times: $360 \div 4 = 90$, so turn 90 degrees.

• An octagon has 8 sides, so the loop runs 8 times: $360 \div 8 = 45$, so turn 45 degrees.

• A triangle has 3 sides, so the loop runs 3 times: $360 \div 3 = ?$

STEP 4 – ROUND IN CIRCLES

⇨ We can make a polygon that looks like a circle by increasing the number of sides. Modify your code like this:

```
polygons.py
import turtle
for s in range(36):
    turtle.lt(10)
    turtle.fd(15)
```

⇨ **Save** and **Run** your code.

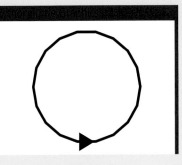

STEP 5 – POLYGON PATTERNS

⇨ Use two loops to repeat the pattern. This is called **nesting** loops. You can change the speed of the turtle by giving it a value from 1 (slow) to 10 (fast). The number 0 often does strange things in coding. In this case, it makes the turtle go faster! Delete your code and add the following:

⇨ Python will try to help by indenting your code. If your code does not indent automatically, make sure you indent so that your code is displayed exactly as in the **IDLE Editor** box here. Then **Save** and **Run** your code.

```
polygons.py
import turtle
turtle.speed(0)
for p in range(10):
    turtle.fd(15)
    for s in range(36):
        turtle.lt(10)
        turtle.fd(15)
```

Prepare the graphics library.
Make the turtle move faster.
Repeat the pattern 10 times.
Move the turtle 15 steps between each circle.
Draw a circle.

STEP 6 – TURN AGAIN

⇨ Now try turning a few degrees between each circle using the following code:

```
polygons.py
import turtle
turtle.speed(0)
for p in range(24):
    turtle.rt(15)
    for s in range(36):
        turtle.lt(10)
        turtle.fd(15)
```

Change the **for p** loop to run 24 times.

Change **turtle.fd(15)** to **turtle.rt(15)**.

 Save and **Run** your code.

CUSTOMIZE
• Make your own shapes and patterns.

> ROLL THE DIE

When we are creating a computer game, we need to add an element of surprise to keep the player guessing what will happen. To do this, we use random numbers. These are unpredictable numbers that are made up by the computer. To use random numbers in Python, we need to work with another library.

STEP 1 – PICK A NUMBER ▶

⇨ Run **IDLE** and start a new file.

⇨ Type in the following code:

```
Untitled
import random
print(random.randint(1,10))
```

Bring in the random library.

Print a random number between 1 and 10. The letters "int" in the code stand for integer, which means whole number.

⇨ Type **numbers** as the filename.

⇨ **Run** your code a few times. Which random numbers do you get?

Python ..
Run Module

```
Python 3.5 Shell
>>>
8
>>>
3
>>>
9
>>>
```

STEP 2 – PLANNING ▶

Now, we are going to extend our program to create a large die that is drawn on the screen and shows a different random number each time it is run. Before we begin, let's start with some planning. We need to:

1. Import the libraries we need.

2. Draw a big colored square.

3. Pick a random number.

4. Print the number on the square in a large font size.

In this activity, use the filename **numbers**. Never give one of your Python files the name **random**, or it will confuse Python and stop it from working properly.

So far, we have used the print command to write numbers in the Python console. To make the numbers appear larger, we can use the **turtle.write()** command.

The font name, inside quotes.

Two closing brackets: one for the font, one for the write command.

```
turtle.write('Hi', font=('Arial', 60, 'normal'))
```

The text we want the turtle to write.

Type **font=** followed by a left bracket.

The font size.

Font style: normal, bold, or italic.

STEP 3 – CODE THE DIE ▶

⇨ Delete your code from step 1 and type in the code below. Make sure the lines are indented (or not indented) exactly as shown. You may have to do this manually.

⇨ **Run** your code a few times. Which numbers do you get on your die?

numbers.py

```
import turtle                Bring in the turtle library.
import random                Bring in the random library.
turtle.speed(0)              Make the turtle move quickly.
turtle.color('red')          Set the color of the die.
turtle.begin_fill()          Prepare Python to fill in any shapes.
for n in range(4):           Start a loop that runs 4 times:
    turtle.forward(100)          Move the turtle forward.
    turtle.right(90)             Turn the turtle right 90 degrees.
turtle.end_fill()            Fill in the previously drawn shape (the square).
turtle.pu()                  Stop the turtle drawing lines.
d=random.randint(1,6)        Make a variable called d, storing a random number.
turtle.color('white')        Set the color of the die number.
turtle.goto(30,-80)          Set where to draw the die number.
turtle.write(d, font=('Arial', 60, 'normal')) Write the die number on the die.
```

CUSTOMIZE

• Experiment with different numbers in the **randint** command.

• Try changing the color of the die, the text, and the font name.

• Can you add a second die to your program?

> GUESS THE NUMBER

We can create a simple guessing game using random numbers. The computer will "think" of a random number that the player has to guess. Each time the player guesses a number, the computer will give a clue by saying if the number is too high, too low, or correct.

STEP 1 – THINK OF A NUMBER ▶

⇨ Run **IDLE** and start a new file.
⇨ Type in the following code:

```
Untitled
import random
n=random.randint(1,20)
print(n)
```

Import the random library.
Pick a random number between 1 and 20, then store it in a variable called **n**.
Display the number.

STEP 2 – SAVE AND RUN ▶

⇨ Type **guessing** as the filename.

⇨ **Run** your code a few times to test it.

mat **Run** Optio

Python ..
Run Module

```
Python 3.5 Shell
>>>
17
>>>
3
>>>
12
>>>
```

STEP 3 – ASK THE PLAYER TO GUESS ▶

Now that we know the computer can think of a number, we need to ask the player to try to guess it. We will use an **input** command to do this. An input command asks the person using the program to type something in. Whatever they type in gets stored in a variable.

⇨ Modify your code by deleting the last line and adding this **input** command:

Make sure you put quotes around your text and brackets at the beginning and end.

```
Untitled
import random
n=random.randint(1,20)
g=input('Guess my number ')
```

Put a space before the second quote.

⇨ **Save** and **Run** your code to test it again.

STEP 4 – RIGHT OR WRONG?

⇨ Next, we need the computer to tell us if the player's guess was correct or not. If the guess was wrong, then we need the player to keep guessing. If it was correct, we can congratulate the player! To do this, we will use a command called **while**. This will make the program keep looping while the guess is wrong. Change your code to the following:

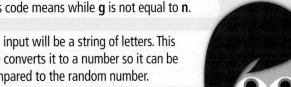

guessing.py

```
import random
n=random.randint(1,20)
g=0
while(g!=n):
  g=input('Guess my number ')
  g=int(g)
print('Correct!')
```

The variable **g** will store the player's guess. Set it to 0 to start.

This code means while **g** is not equal to **n**.

The input will be a string of letters. This line converts it to a number so it can be compared to the random number.

⇨ **Save** and **Run** your code to test it again. Guess a number each time the program asks you to. When you eventually guess the right number, it will say **Correct!**

STEP 5 – GIVE ME A CLUE!

⇨ The game will be more entertaining if we can give the player a clue. We can do this by checking to see if the number is too high or too low. This code needs something called an IF statement. An IF statement can tell if something is true or not, then run different pieces of code depending on the answer. Change your code to the following:

guessing.py

```
import random

n=random.randint(1,20)
g=0

while(g!=n):
  g=input('Guess my number ')
  g=int(g)
  if(g>n):
     print('Too big')
  if(g<n):
     print('Too small')
print('Correct!')
```

Bring in the random library.

Set the variable **n** to a random number.
Set the variable **g** to 0.

Keep looping while the guess is wrong.
Input a new guess.
Turn it into a number.
If **g** is greater than **n**:
Tell the player their guess is too big.
If **g** is less than **n**:
Tell them their guess is too small.
When **g** equals **n** (the guess equals the random number): display **Correct!**

KEY CONCEPTS

WHILE COMMAND
A while command keeps looping some code while something is true.

IF STATEMENT
An IF statement runs some code if a particular condition is true.

Save and **Run** your code to test it again.
Have fun playing it, and try it out on a friend!

> RANDOM PATTERNS

We are going to create a program that makes a random piece of art. Using a loop, we will draw multiple lines on the screen in random positions. To make the lines different colors, we will pick from a list of colors at random.

STEP 1 – PLAN THE PROGRAM ▷

⇨ Import the libraries we need.

⇨ Make a list of colors.

⇨ Start a loop.

⇨ Pick random **x** and **y** values for the end point of the line you have drawn.

⇨ Pick a random color from the list.

⇨ Draw a line in the chosen color to the random end point.

STEP 2 – LEARN ABOUT LISTS ▷

We will use a list of colors as part of the program. First, let's look at how Python handles lists. We have already used variables to store single pieces of data. A list extends this to store multiple pieces of data. A list could include things such as days of the week, people's names, or the locations of objects in a game.

Separate each item in the list with a comma.

The list contains text strings (words), so put quotes around each item.

⇨ Run **IDLE** and start a new file.

⇨ Type in the following code:

```
Untitled
import random
cols=['blue','green','red','yellow']
print(random.choice(cols))
```

The list must start and end with square brackets [ ].

random.choice tells Python to return an item at random from the list inside the brackets. We call it a *function*.

Make sure you use all the brackets required. We need two sets at the end: one for the choice function, one for the print command.

STEP 3 – SAVE AND RUN

⇨ Type **lines** as the filename.

⇨ **Save** your code.

⇨ **Run** your code a few times.

```
Python 3.5 Shell
>>>
green
>>>
yellow
>>>
blue
>>>
```

LIST

To store several pieces of data, use a list. Programmers sometimes call a list like this an *array*.

STEP 4 – THE MAIN CODE

⇨ Change your code to create this program. Add blank line spaces between your code to make it clearer to read:

lines.py

```
import turtle
import random

cols=['blue','green','red','yellow']

turtle.speed(0)

for c in range(100):
  x=random.randint(-200,200)
  y=random.randint(-200,200)
  turtle.color(random.choice(cols))
  turtle.goto(x,y)
```

Bring in the turtle library.

Bring in the random library.

Make a list of colors, called **cols**.

Make the turtle move quickly.

Start a loop that runs 100 times.

Make variables called **x** and **y** with random values from -200 to 200.

Set the turtle to a random color.

Move the turtle to random *coordinates* (x, y).

CUSTOMIZE

- Try increasing the number of lines that are drawn.

- Why not try adding more colors to the list?

- Experiment with the maximum and minimum random values for **x** and **y**.

- Change the thickness of the lines by adding the **turtle. pensize(8)** command.

> TURTLE RACE

Python is very good at doing calculations. It can also be used to make simple games. In this activity, we will create multiple turtles and program them to move across the screen at random speeds.

STEP 1 – PLAN THE GAME ▶

⇨ Import the libraries we need.

⇨ Make three turtles.

⇨ Set their colors.

⇨ Change their shape from a triangle to a large turtle icon.

⇨ Move them to the start position.

⇨ Start a loop for the race.

⇨ Move each turtle forward a small, random amount during each loop.

STEP 2 – MAKE THREE TURTLES ▶

We need to make three turtles and give each one a name. To keep things simple, we will call them **a**, **b**, and **c**. They will all begin from the same starting line, which is an **x** variable, so we need to move each one to a different **y** location.

⇨ Run **IDLE** and start a new file. Type in the following code:

```
untitled
import turtle
import random

a = turtle.Turtle()
b = turtle.Turtle()
c = turtle.Turtle()

a.goto(-300,-100)
b.goto(-300,0)
c.goto(-300,100)
```

Import the libraries we need.

Create the three turtles called **a**, **b**, and **c**.

Move each of them to different coordinates. Notice they have the same **x** variable, and different **y** variables.

⇨ **Save** and **Run** your code to test it so far. Call your file **race**. You should see your three turtles as arrows.

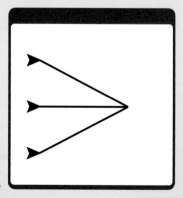

⇨ Carefully change your code so it looks like the following program.
Check your code for errors by looking at the patterns between **a**, **b**, and **c**.

race.py

```
import turtle
import random

a = turtle.Turtle()
a.color('red')

b = turtle.Turtle()
b.color('blue')

c = turtle.Turtle()
c.color('purple')

turtle = [a, b, c]

for item in turtle:
    item.penup()
    item.shape('turtle')
    item.shapesize(4)

a.goto(-300,-100)
b.goto(-300,0)
c.goto(-300,100)

for race in range(100):
    for item in turtle:
        item.fd(random.randint(0,12))
```

Import the libraries we need.

Make a turtle called **a** and color it red.

Make a turtle called **b** and color it blue.

Make a turtle called **c** and color it purple.

Make a list of the turtles we are using. The turtles are not text strings, so don't use any quotes!

Loop through each of the items in the list.
Stop the turtles from drawing with **penup()**.
Make them turtle-shaped instead of triangular.
Stretch them so they are four times bigger.

Move each of them to different coordinates.

Make the race last 100 loops.
Loop through each of the turtles in the list.
Move each one forward a random number of steps.

 Save and **Run** your code.

CUSTOMIZE

• Change the color of the turtles.

• Make them move more quickly or more slowly.

• Add more turtles.

› KEYBOARD SKETCHER

The turtle in Python can be programmed to do different things when different keyboard keys are pressed. By making the turtle move up when someone presses the up arrow and down when they press down, we can make a simple drawing program. In this way, we are defining a *procedure*: creating a new super-command that combines other commands.

STEP 1 – PLAN THE PROGRAM

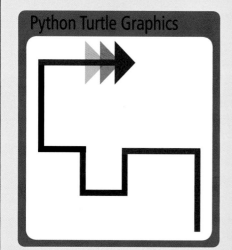

Python Turtle Graphics

⇨ Import the libraries we need.

⇨ Set the line width (or **pensize**).

⇨ When the **left** keyboard arrow is pressed, face left and move 20 steps.

⇨ When the **right** arrow is pressed, face right and move 20 steps.

⇨ When the **up** arrow is pressed, face the top of the screen and move up 20 steps.

⇨ When the **down** arrow is pressed, face the bottom of the screen and move down 20 steps.

⇨ When **r** is pressed, change to red. When **g** is pressed, change to green. (Other colors can be added later.)

STEP 2 – START DRAWING

We need to define a new command that will make the turtle move and draw up the screen. Programmers call this defining a procedure. Each time the **up** arrow is pressed, we will run this procedure.

⇨ Run **IDLE** and start a new file. Type in the following code:

Import the turtle library.

```
Untitled
import turtle

def drawUp():
  turtle.seth(90)
  turtle.fd(20)
turtle.onkey(drawUp,'Up')

turtle.listen()
```

Define a procedure called **drawUp**. Make sure you include the brackets () and colon.

Indent the code you want to run when the procedure is used: **seth(90)** makes the turtle face the top of the screen.

Tell the turtle to run the procedure whenever the **up** arrow is pressed.

Make sure the turtle is "listening" to the keyboard and will notice keys being pressed.

STEP 3 – TEST YOUR CODE

⇨ **Save** and **Run** your code to test it so far. Call your file **sketch**.

⇨ Click the turtle graphics screen first to make sure the key presses are noticed by the turtle.

⇨ Press the **up** arrow key.

STEP 4 – THE MAIN CODE

⇨ Once you have one key working, carefully change your code to the following:

sketch.py

```
import turtle
turtle.pensize(5)

def drawUp():
    turtle.seth(90)
    turtle.fd(20)

def drawDown():
    turtle.seth(270)
    turtle.fd(20)

def drawLeft():
    turtle.seth(180)
    turtle.fd(20)

def drawRight():
    turtle.seth(0)
    turtle.fd(20)

def setRed():
    turtle.color('Red')

def setGreen():
    turtle.color('Green')

turtle.onkey(drawUp,'Up')
turtle.onkey(drawDown,'Down')
turtle.onkey(drawLeft,'Left')
turtle.onkey(drawRight,'Right')

turtle.onkey(setRed,'r')
turtle.onkey(setGreen,'g')

turtle.listen()
```

Draw a thicker line.

Define a procedure to draw a line up the screen.

Define a procedure to draw a line down the screen.

Define a procedure to draw a line to the left.

Define a procedure to draw a line to the right.

Define a procedure to draw in red.

Define a procedure to draw in green.

Tell the turtle to run the appropriate procedure when each arrow key is pressed.

Tell the turtle to notice the keys being pressed.

CUSTOMIZE

- Add other procedures to change to other colors.

- Make another procedure that changes the pen width.

KEY CONCEPT

FUNCTION

A function is a type of procedure or routine that returns a value back to the main code.

 Save and **Run** your code. Now try to sketch with the arrow keys. What cool patterns can you create with your new program?

> THE CLOCK

This program makes a clock face with moving hour, minute, and second hands. The time library is used to find out the real time, and an interval *timer* is used to draw the hands in the correct place every second.

STEP 1 – FIND THE TIME ▶

⇨ Run **IDLE** and start a new file. Type in the following code:

```
Untitled
import time
t= time.localtime()
print(t)
```

Import the time library.

Find the local time and store it in the variable **t**.

Print the time.

⇨ **Save** your code. Name it **clock**.

⇨ **Run** the code and you should see the time is broken down into the year, month, day, hour, minute, and so on, like this:

```
Python 3.5 Shell
>>>
== RESTART: clock.py ===
time.struct_time(tm_year=2017, tm_mon=9,
tm_mday=6, tm_hour=14, tm_min=22, tm_sec=59,
tm_wday=1, tm_yday=250, tm_isdst=1)
>>>
```

STEP 2 – DIGITAL CLOCK ▶

⇨ We don't need to know the day or year. Modify your code in the following way, so it shows the hours, minutes, and seconds only. **Save** and **Run** your code.

```
clock.py
import time
t= time.localtime()
print(t.tm_hour, t.tm_min, t.tm_sec)
```

STEP 3 – SOME PLANS AND CALCULATIONS ▶

We can use three different turtles—one for each of the hands on the clock:

The second hand will rotate 360 *degrees* once every 60 seconds. 360 ÷ 60 = 6, so it must rotate 6 degrees every second.

The minute hand rotates 360 degrees every 60 minutes, so we can multiply the minutes by 6 to get the angle it should be shown at.

The hour hand turns 360 degrees once every 12 hours. 360 ÷ 12 = 30, so we need to multiply the number of hours by 30 to get the angle of the hour hand.

When it is 3:30, the hour hand should be between the 3 and the 4, so we also need to turn the hour hand an extra 30 degrees every 60 minutes (half a degree a minute).

We will change the color, shape, and size of each of the clock's hands:

The minute hand will be a black turtle called **m**. It will be longer than the hour hand, but slightly shorter than the second hand.

The second hand will be a red turtle called **s**. It needs to be the longest hand.

The hour hand will be a blue turtle called **h**. It needs to be short.

STEP 4 – MAIN CODE ▶

⇨ Type in the following code:

```python
import turtle
import time

turtle.mode('logo')

h = turtle.Turtle()
h.color('blue')
h.shape('arrow')
h.shapesize(1,10)

m = turtle.Turtle()
m.color('black')
m.shape('arrow')
m.shapesize(1,14)

s = turtle.Turtle()
s.color('red')
s.shape('arrow')
s.shapesize(1,15)

def showHands():
    t=time.localtime()
    s.seth(t.tm_sec*6)
    m.seth(t.tm_min*6)
    h.seth(t.tm_hour*30 + t.tm_min*0.5)
    turtle.ontimer(showHands, 1000)

showHands()
```

Import the libraries we need.

Set the turtle mode to **logo**. This makes sure it measures angles in a clockwise direction.

Create the hour hand.
Make the hand blue.
Make the hand arrow-shaped.
Make the hand 10 times longer than normal.

Create the minute hand.
Make the hand black.
Make the hand arrow-shaped.
Make the hand 14 times longer than normal.

Create the second hand.
Make the hand red.
Make the hand arrow-shaped.
Make the hand 15 times longer than normal.

Define a procedure to draw the hands.
Store the time in the variable **t.**
Set the angle of the second hand.
Set the angle of the minute hand.
Set the angle of the hour hand.
Make the procedure run itself again after 1000 milliseconds (1 second later).
Run the **showHands** procedure.

Save and **Run** your code. Watch your clock display the correct time, then turn the page and find out how to display the time in a clock face.

STEP 5 – FURTHER PLANNING

We have a working clock, but to make it useful we need to give it a clock face.
By using loops and drawing commands, we can add a face to our clock.

 ⇨ Start by drawing a large black dot in the centre of the screen.

 ⇨ Draw a white dot on top of the black dot to make a ring around the edge of the clock.

 ⇨ Draw 60 markings around the edge of the clock—one for every minute, every 5 degrees.

 ⇨ Draw 12 larger hour markings around the edge of the clock—one for every hour, every 30 degrees.

STEP 6 – MAKE SPACE

⇨ We need to make space for the code to draw the clock face. Click to start adding code before the **showHands()** command near the end of your program.

⇨ Press **enter** a few times to make some space.

 turtle.ontimer(showHands, 1000)

 Click here and press **enter**.

 showHands( )

TIMER
To make something happen after a delay, use the **turtle.ontimer** command.

STEP 7 – DEFINE THE FACE

⇨ Type the following code into the gap you created in step 6:

clock.py

```
def makeFace():
    b=turtle.Turtle()
    b.speed(0)
    b.hideturtle()
    b.penup()

    b.dot(350)
    b.pencolor('white')
    b.dot(340)

    b.pencolor('black')
    for a in range(0,360,6):
        b.goto(0,0)
        b.seth(a)
        b.fd(160)
        b.dot(5)

    for a in range(0,360,30):
        b.goto(0,0)
        b.seth(a)
        b.fd(160)
        b.dot(10)
```

	Define the procedure to draw the clock face.
	Make a new turtle to draw the background.
	Draw the clock face quickly.
	Hide the turtle.
	Stop the turtle from drawing a line.
	Make a big black circle for the edge.
	Change color.
	Create a big white circle for the clock face.
	Change the color back to black.
	Start a loop to draw the minute dots.
	Move turtle **b** to the center.
	Turn it to the angle for each minute dot.
	Move the turtle to the edge.
	Mark a small dot.
	Start a loop to draw the hour dots.
	Move turtle **b** to the center.
	Turn it to the angle for each hour dot.
	Move the turtle to the edge.
	Mark a dot.

STEP 8 – DRAW THE FACE

⇨ We have told Python how to draw the clock face by defining the procedure, but we haven't told it to draw it yet!

⇨ Type in **makeFace()** at the end of your program, just before the line that says **showHands()**.

→ b.dot(10)

makeFace()

→ showHands()

 Now, test your code and watch your clock tell the time!

CUSTOMIZE

• Why not change the color of the clock or the clock hands?

• You could experiment with dot colors and multiple dots.

• If you want to add numbers to the clock, you will need to use the **turtle.write** command:

```
for a in range(1,13):
    b.goto(0,0)
    b.seth(a*30)
    b.fd(140)
    b.write(a)
```

⟨25⟩

› HANGMAN

In the game Hangman, the computer "thinks" of a word. The player then has to guess the word by choosing one letter at a time. The computer needs to check to see if the letter is in the word, and to let the player know if it is.

As this is a more complex program, we need to plan it carefully. The steps to make a program work are called an *algorithm*.

STEP 1 – PLANNING

⇨ Pick a random word from a list: House, Apple, Pizza, Round, Green.

To make it easier to code and harder to guess, we will choose words that are all five letters long.

Each item in the list will be a text string, so each will need quotes around it. Separate each one with a comma.

⇨ Keep looping until the word is guessed:

Show the word so far.   Ask for a letter.

* * * * *   S

If the letter is in the word, show the player where.

If the guess is incorrect, tell the player it's not in the word.

✗

⇨ We will need to check each letter in the word to see if the suggested letter is there.

To find a specific letter in a word or text string, we can treat it like a numbered list. So, if the variable called word is **HOUSE**, then **word[0]** will return the answer **H**, **word[1]** will return the answer **O**, **word[2]** will be **U**, and so on.

⇨ Run **IDLE** and start a new file. Type in the following code:

Untitled

```python
import random

wordList=['HOUSE','APPLE','PIZZA','ROUND','GREEN']
word=random.choice(wordList)
guess='*****'

while(guess!=word):
    print('Here is the word',guess)
    letter=input('Guess a letter')
    hasLetter=False
    newguess=[]

    for n in range(5):
        if(letter==word[n]):
            newguess.append(letter)
            hasLetter=True
        else:
            newguess.append(guess[n])

    guess=''.join(newguess)

    if(hasLetter==True):
        print('Good guess')
    else:
        print('Not in the word')

print('The word was',word)
```

Import the random library.

List possible words.
Make a variable called **guess** to store the word as letters are guessed.

Loop until all letters have been guessed.
　Print the letters guessed so far.
　Ask the player for a letter.
　Start by assuming it is not in the word.
　Make a list to show any new guesses.

Start a loop for each letter in the word.
　If the guess is one of the letters:
　　add it to the **newguess** list
　　make a note that it has the letter.
If not in the word:
　add an asterisk * .

Join the list of letters as a string and store them in the guess variable. There are two single quotation marks after the equal sign.
　If the guess is one of the letters:
　　tell the player.
　If not:
　　tell the player.

If the word has been guessed correctly, leave the **while** loop and tell the player.

⇨ **Save** and **Run** your code. Name it **hangman**.

Try your game out with a friend. Remember, Python won't recognize lowercase letters when a capital letter has been used.

CUSTOMIZE

• Try adding more possible words for the computer to pick. They all need to be five letters long. Make sure you use single quotation marks for each one and separate them with commas.

• Change all the words for longer words—but make sure that they are still the same length. You will also need to change the number of times the loop runs to make sure each letter is checked: once for each letter in the word.

Python Turtle Graphics

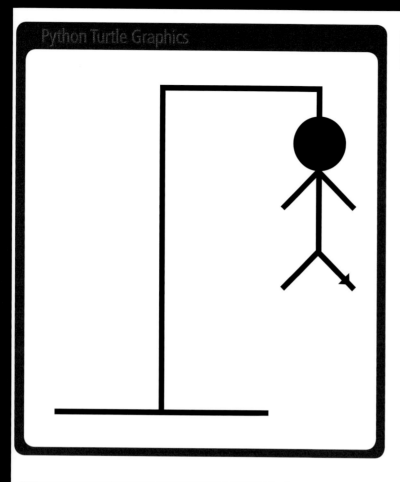

STEP 3 – MAKE SPACE ▶

⇨ We can make the hangman game much more interesting by adding graphics.

⇨ You need to add some new code. Click to move the cursor before the **while** command in your code.

⇨ Press **enter** a few times to make some space.

STEP 4 – DRAW THE STICK MAN ▶

⇨ Type the following code into your program between **guess** and **while**:

➡ `guess='*****'`

```python
import random
import turtle
turtle.pensize(5)
errors=0

def showStickman():
    if(errors==1):
        turtle.bk(100)
        turtle.fd(200)
    if(errors==2):
        turtle.bk(100)
        turtle.lt(90)
        turtle.fd(300)
    if(errors==3):
        turtle.rt(90)
        turtle.fd(150)
    if(errors==4):
        turtle.rt(90)
        turtle.fd(50)
    if(errors==5):
        turtle.dot(50)
    if(errors==6):
        turtle.fd(100)
        turtle.bk(75)
    if(errors==7):
        turtle.rt(45)
        turtle.fd(50)
        turtle.bk(50)
    if(errors==8):
        turtle.lt(90)
        turtle.fd(50)
        turtle.bk(50)
    if(errors==9):
        turtle.rt(45)
        turtle.fd(75)
        turtle.rt(45)
        turtle.fd(50)
        turtle.bk(50)
    if(errors==10):
        turtle.lt(90)
        turtle.fd(50)
```

➡ `while(guess!=word):`

<28>

STEP 5 – LIMIT THE GUESSES ▶

⇨ Change the **while** command so it also checks to make sure no more than 10 errors have been made while guessing:

```
while((guess!=word)and(errors<10)):
```

STEP 6 – COUNT AND DRAW ▶

⇨ Find the command near the end of the program that says **print('Not in the word')**. Add two new lines of code below this. The first keeps count of the incorrect guesses (errors); the second runs the procedure that draws the stick man:

```
→ print('Not in the word')
  errors=errors+1
  showStickman()
```

HOW IT WORKS ▶

Every time the player makes an incorrect guess, the **errors** variable is increased by one. When the **showStickman** procedure runs, it uses a series of IF statements to find which part of the stick man to draw. Each of the IF statements draws a different part:

errors = 1   errors = 2   errors = 3

errors = 4   errors = 5   errors = 6

errors = 7   errors = 8   errors = 9   errors = 10

CUSTOMIZE

• Modify the hangman graphics. Try making them all much bigger so they fill the screen. Add colors.

• Alter the code so that each time the player gets a letter wrong, the number of incorrect guesses is shown.

• Use the **.upper()** function to make sure all the letters that are guessed get turned into capitals. You need to add a line that says **letter=letter.upper()** after the letter is set by the input command.

› GLOSSARY

ALGORITHM Rules or steps followed to do something

ARRAY Series of numbers or words stored as a list

BUG An error in a program that stops it from working properly

COMMAND A special word that tells a computer to do something

COORDINATES The position of the turtle using **x** and **y** values to describe how far across and up it is from the center

DEBUG To remove bugs, or errors, from a program

DEGREES The units used to measure angles

FUNCTION A procedure that returns a value back to the main code

LIBRARY A collection of extra commands that can be borrowed to use in a program

LOOP An action that repeats one or more commands a number of times

PROCEDURE Several commands that do something when combined

RANDOM NUMBER A number that can't be predicted

STEPS Small movements made by the turtle

STRING A sequence of variables, such as names or numbers

TIMER A command that runs another function after a specified delay

TURTLE An object that moves around the screen when given specific commands

VARIABLE A value that can change: used to store information in a program

UNDERSTANDING ERROR MESSAGES

When you run a program that has some bugs, Python will try to help you by giving you some clues. The text that shows up in the **console** may look hard to understand, but look carefully. Python explains where and what the error is.

```
PYTHON 3.5 Shell
File 'my new program.py', line 1, in <module>
        print(a)
NameError: name 'a' is not defined
>>>
```

The bug is in line 1 of the program, right at the start.

You have tried to print the variable **a** before giving it a value.

```
PYTHON 3.5 Shell
clock.py",line 18, in showHands
        turtle.forwad(150)
AttributeError: module 'turtle' has no attribute 'forwad'
>>>
```

The error is in line 18 of the program.

turtle.forward has a missing letter!

‹30›

› BUGS AND DEBUGGING ‹

COMMON BUGS WHEN USING PYTHON

When you find your code is not working as expected, stop and look through each command you have put in. Think about what you want the command to do, and what it is really telling the computer to do. If you are entering one of the programs in this book, check that you have not missed a line. Some things to watch out for:

Type commands carefully:

```
prnt(123)
```

```
print(123)
```

Spell them properly!

Add quotes:

```
print('OK)
```

```
print('OK')
```

Use quotes at each end.

Check for capitals:

```
Print(123)
```

```
print(123)
```

Python is "case-sensitive."

Add brackets:

```
print(123
```

```
print(123)
```

Use open and closed brackets.

Watch for color changes

Many commands change color when you type them correctly.

When you add a second quote to a string, the string will change color.

Watch carefully while coding, and the color will help keep your code error free.

Indentation

```
for n in range (5):
    print('A')
    print('B')
print('C')
```

Every line of code you want to include in a loop needs to be indented. If you want something to happen after the loop, make sure it is not indented.

Remember to finish a **for**, **def**, or **while** command with a colon (:).

Look for patterns

As you are typing in code, look for patterns. Try looking up and down the page, not just left to right. Is there a line of code that looks very different from the others? A bug may be lurking there.

TIPS TO REDUCE BUGS

🐛 If you are making your own program, spend time drawing a diagram and planning it before you start. Try changing values if things don't work, and don't be afraid to start again—you will learn from it.

🐛 Practice debugging! Make a short program and get a friend to change one line of code while you're not looking. Can you fix it?

Libraries

Remember to import the libraries you need.

```
import turtle
```
← Any program using graphics.
```
import random
```
← Any program needing random numbers or random choices.
```
import time
```
← Any program where you need to know the time.

For more information about Python visit www.python.org

‹31›

INDEX